The Twelve Pillars of the Christian Faith

Frederick Serjeant

The Twelve Doctrines – basic teachings from the Bible that uphold the only true Gospel of Salvation

A Personal Letter

Frederick Serjeant
f.serjeant@gmai.com
Dorset
England
Date: Today

Dear You (whoever You are)

What a wonderful gift the Internet is! It means I can write to everyone in the world and it costs me nothing in postage!

If, like me, you get to turn past the age of ninety, you must surely then realise that you may not be much longer in this world. Now that can be a sad or a happy thought. It depends on whether you have come to know my best friend or not.

Now it is quite possible that when you read this, you may think that I am going to get all 'religious'. But you'd be wrong! I gave up religion years ago. I did not begin that way, but as a young man I became very religious. I even became a priest. No! I am not going to persuade you to be religious. However, I do want to say something about faith.

In my book called 'The Twelve Pillars of the Christian Faith' I present what some may think of as strong "doctrines". But my purpose is really to introduce you to my best friend. That friend is no less a person than Jesus of Nazareth.

How did I come to know Him? It was and is, by faith. If you read The Twelve Pillars, hopefully you will discover how faith is given and how my friend may become your friend as well.

The fact that you or I may not have much longer in this world will possibly be sad for those we love, but a wonderfully happy thought for you and me, because our best friend is waiting to welcome us into his home in glory for all eternity.

Yours ever,

Frederick

Dedication

I dedicate this book to my dear wife Mary, who for 60 years, with constant love, has supported and accompanied me as I have learnt and taught the truths found in its pages.

Most quotations from the Bible, are from the New King James Version.

Scripture taken from the New King James Version®. Copyright © 1982 by Thomas Nelson. Used by permission. All rights reserved.

This book Copyright © 2018 F J Serjeant

For You are my hope, O Lord God;
You are my trust from my youth.
By You I have been upheld from birth;
You are He who took me out of my mother's womb.
My praise shall be continually of You.
I have become as a wonder to many,
But You are my strong refuge.
Let my mouth be filled with Your praise
And with Your glory all the day.
…. I will hope continually,
And will praise You yet more and more.
My mouth shall tell of Your righteousness
And Your salvation all the day,
For I do not know their limits.
I will go in the strength of the Lord God;
I will make mention of Your righteousness, of Yours only.
O God, You have taught me from my youth;
And to this day I declare Your wondrous works.
Now also when I am old and grey-headed,
O God, do not forsake me,
Until I declare Your strength to this generation,
Your power to everyone who is to come.
Also Your righteousness, O God, is very high,
You who have done great things;
O God, who is like You?
…My lips shall greatly rejoice when I sing to You,
And my soul, which You have redeemed.
My tongue also shall talk of Your righteousness all the day long.

From Psalm 71 NKJV

Table of Contents

Chapter 1 Introduction 9

Chapter 2 Pillar 1 The Sovereignty of God..............................15

Chapter 3 Pillar 2 The Gospel of Grace....................................27

Chapter 4 The Five Solas - The Next Five Pillars 35

Chapter 5 Pillar 3 1. SOLA SCRIPTURA (Scriptures alone) 39

Chapter 6 Pillar 4 2. SOLA GRATIA (By Grace alone)...............45

Chapter 7 Pillar 5 3. SOLA FIDE (Through Faith alone) 51

Chapter 8 Pillar 6 4. SOLUS CHRISTUS (In Christ alone)..........57

Chapter 9 Pillar 7 5. SOLI DEO GLORIA (Glory of God alone)...65

Chapter 10 The Doctrines of Grace - The next Five Pillars 71

Chapter 11 Pillar 8 The First Doctrine of Grace 79
"Total Depravity".. 79

Chapter 12 Pillar 9 The Second Doctrine of Grace 85
"Unconditional Election".. 85

Chapter 13 Pillar 10 The Third Doctrine of Grace 93
"Limited Atonement"... 93

Chapter 14 Pillar 11 The Fourth Doctrine of Grace 101
"Invincible Grace" 101

Chapter 15 Pillar 12 The Fifth Doctrine of Grace 111
"The Perseverance of the Saints" 111

Chapter 16 Conclusion 121

Appendix A - A General Statement of Faith 129

Appendix B Some Definitions: 131

Appendix C The Sovereignty Of God

A Collection of Scriptures on this topic 133

The Author 141

Chapter 1

Introduction

Pillars support a structure.. In this book I want to show from the Bible twelve basic doctrines that, like pillars, support the one central message concerning the Kingdom of God as proclaimed and brought in by Jesus Christ.

If you are an enquirer about the Christian Faith, or you are a new disciple, then this book is for you. It may even be that you have regarded yourself as having been a Christian for many years, but are still hazy or confused about some of the key doctrines of the Faith - then this book is also for you.

In **Appendix A**, at the end of the book, I have listed in a brief **'Statement of Faith'** those doctrines that all those who call themselves **'evangelical** [1] Christians generally believe. Please take a look at the Statement before you read on in the chapter, for the following reason:

I am going to take it for granted that you accept and agree with the beliefs briefly set out in that Statement. In a way, we shall be looking at the **background** of these beliefs in these Twelve Pillars. If you have a problem with accepting any part of the 'Statement of Faith', it may be that the following chapters, though they are not be dealing directly with them, may yet clarify any issues you may have concerning them.

Another thought before we proceed. It is important that you do not allow yourself to be put off by the words 'doctrine' or 'theology'. Doctrine merely means 'teachings' – and is used especially to mean 'important special teachings'. 'Theology', just means the study of God and things relating to God.

As in every other particular area of study, you will find special vocabulary used. When the meaning of any special word is used, which perhaps is not obvious, then I will mark the word when it is **first** used, with an asterisk like this*. At the end of

---

[1] By 'evangelicals' we refer to those who hold to the gospel and to the Bible as the word of God – as distinct from 'liberals' and 'Catholics' and others.

the book these words will be explained in a list of definitions in **Appendix B.**

In the chapters that follow, as I have already suggested, you will be introduced to what are seen to be the twelve basic doctrines that explain and support that central message concerning Jesus Christ, which is known as the **Gospel of grace**. This will be explained further, in due course.

You should also be warned from the start of two more things. The first is that you must be prepared for your present way of thinking about Christianity to be radically changed. The second is that **all** Twelve Pillars stand or fall together. (Sometimes called the domino effect). Each Pillar, or doctrine, is related to all the others. Any idea that one can 'cherry-pick' – to believe or accept *some* of the Pillars but reject others - as some today seem to want to do, will not secure their purpose. If you are to grasp the truth that secures a true relationship with God, then **all** Twelve are needful.

At the end of most of the chapters, I have added a well known Hymn. The Hymns are put there for meditation and prayer.. They have been chosen to express in song - where possible - the teaching contained in that chapter. If the reader is unfamiliar with the Hymns, the tunes for them can usually be found by searching online. You will remember more of the teaching if you learn to sing them by heart!

> **A Key Question:** If you were to die tonight and found yourself before God – and God asked you **"Why should I let you into my heaven?"** How would you answer?

You might want to give a different answer when you have read this book!

So let's make a start with the First Pillar.

Chapter 2

Pillar 1

The Sovereignty of God

Throughout all the chapters, I shall be noting or quoting Bible references – Book, Chapter, verse(s) [2]. It is very important that the reader should have a Bible to hand and that he/she looks up those references and read each in its **context** – that is, the verses that go before and after it. It is very easy for someone to take texts out of their contexts and distort their meaning. So we encourage you to be like the 'Bereans'

---

[2] For example 'John 3:16' refers to the **book** – The Gospel of John, then the **Chapter** 3. Then the **Verse** numbered in that Chapter, namely verse 16. If you look it up now, you will come to the most famous verse in the Bible. It begins with the words, "God so loved the world…."

referred to in Acts 17:11, who "searched the Scriptures daily, to see whether these things were so".

I have a little saying: **"Context is King!"** By that I mean that the context (the place where it is found) of any verse, paragraph, chapter or Book in the Bible, should govern its meaning. Not all books in the Bible are alike. Some are mainly history, some poetry, some prophecy etc. Also, you should ask yourself, is this from the Old or the New Testament? "Who is the speaker? To whom was it or is it being spoken? etc..

If possible, it will also be found helpful to have more than one translation of the Bible, including a modern language version. Actual quotations from the Bible will usually be printed in italics *like this.*

With that in mind, then, we come to our first pillar- "The Sovereignty of God".

If you look up the word 'sovereign' in a dictionary, you will find expressions like: 'superior', 'greatest', 'supreme in power and authority', 'ruler', and 'independent of all others', by way of definition. But in referring to God's sovereignty as revealed in the Scriptures, we may simply state that God is **in total control** of everything throughout time and eternity.

There is absolutely nothing that occurs in the universe that is outside of God's controlling influence, power and authority. God has no limitations. He is omnipotent*[3] and omniscient*. These are two of His eternal unchanging attributes*. They are essential to His nature as God, otherwise, He would not truly be God and certainly not the one true God of the Bible!

Consider just a few of the claims the Bible makes about Him:

God is above all things and before all things. He is the alpha and the omega, the beginning and the end. He is immortal, and He is present everywhere so that everyone can know that He exists (Romans 1:19, Revelation 21:6).

God created all things and holds all things together, both in heaven and on earth, both visible and invisible (Colossians 1:16).

God knows all things past, present, and future. There is no limit to His knowledge, for God knows everything completely before it even happens (Romans 11:33).

God can do all things and accomplish all things. Nothing is too difficult for Him, and He orchestrates and determines

---

[3] Remember that words marked with an asterisk * are explained in Appendix B

everything that is going to happen in your life, in my life, and in the lives of all humanity throughout the world and throughout time and eternity.

Whatever He wants to do in the universe, He does, for nothing is impossible with Him.

Oh, Lord God! You Yourself made the heavens and earth by Your great power and with Your outstretched arm. Nothing is too difficult for You! (Jeremiah 32:17 HCSB).

God is in control of all things and rules over all things. He has power and authority over nature, earthly kings, history, angels, and demons. Even Satan himself has to ask God's permission before he can act (Psalm 103:19).

That's what being sovereign means. It means being the ultimate source of all power, authority, and everything that exists. Only God can make those claims; therefore, it's God's sovereignty that makes Him superior to all other so-called gods and makes Him, and Him alone, worthy of worship.

This is possibly one of the most difficult doctrines that the new, or immature believer, has to come to terms with. For if God is absolutely sovereign as stated here, then it would seem to suggest that He is the author not only of all good things but also of all evil.

The question no doubt arises in many persons' minds, "If God is a good God and if He is also in complete control of all things, how is it that so many bad things happen in the world?"

The apostle Paul points us, (in Chapter 9 of Romans). not to an answer to this question, but to an attitude that we should take in regard to it. He is particularly concerned with the questions of election and predestination*.

"What shall we say then? Is there unrighteousness with God? Certainly not! For He says to Moses, "I will have mercy on whomever I will have mercy, and I will have compassion on whomever I will have compassion." So then it is not of him who wills, nor of him who runs, but of God who shows mercy. For the Scripture says to the Pharaoh, "For this very purpose I have raised you up, that I may show My power in you, and that My name may be declared in all the earth." Therefore He has mercy on whom He wills, and whom He wills He hardens. You will say to me then, "Why does He still find fault? For who has resisted His will?" But indeed, O man, who are you to reply against God? Will the thing formed say to him who formed it, "Why have you made me like this?" Does not the potter have power over the

clay, from the same lump to make one vessel for honour and another for dishonour? What if God, wanting to show His wrath and to make His power known, endured with much longsuffering the vessels of wrath prepared for destruction, and that He might make known the riches of His glory on the vessels of mercy, which He had prepared beforehand for glory, even us whom He called, not of the Jews only, but also of the Gentiles? As He says also in Hosea: "I will call them 'My people', who were not My people, And her 'beloved', who was not beloved.""
Romans 9:14–25 NKJV

This passage from Paul's Letter to the Romans is said by some to be the most difficult passage in all the Bible to accept. But the real test is whether you believe in a sovereign God or not. Is God free to do completely as He chooses? Do you or I know better than God?

What kind of God do you want? One who is helpless to interfere in events of the world, or one who is in charge?

Romans 8:28 declares:

"And we know that all things work together for good to those who love God, to those who are the called according to His purpose." Romans 8:28 NKJV

Only a sovereign God can weave all things together to produce a 'tapestry of good' in your life and mine. What wonderful security belief in a sovereign God gives us!

I realise that some at this point will be wondering how this fits in with the idea of man having "free will". We shall be looking at this a little later. Meanwhile, we would say that all men are able to make choices, but that does not mean they are completely free in the choices they make.

This Pillar is the first starting point. Failure to grasp this truth about God will result in a failure to grasp the truth of all the other eleven pillars.

The question is whether you will, by God's grace, bow the knee – that is, submit to His sovereignty - or not.

Rebellion against the sovereignty of God is what **sin** is. The rebellion of Satan and other angels with him - also the disobedience of Adam and all mankind, is what has brought about all the evil and suffering we find in the world.

But God, in His sovereign purpose, as we shall see, has a wonderful plan of redemption* which He is carrying out through Jesus Christ, His Son. In that plan, the greatest evil of all – the crucifixion of the Son of God, results in the greatest good that one could ever imagine!

The remaining eleven Pillars are all about this wonderful plan of God and how each one may find his or her part in it.

Before we leave this Pillar and move on to Pillar Two, have a look at **Appendix C** at the back of the book. There you will find a larger selection of Scriptures about the Sovereignty of God.

William Cowper

William Cowper. lived from 1731 to 1800. He suffered grievously all his life from severe depression, even to the point of losing his mind for some periods and needing to be cared for in an asylum.. But throughout all his sufferings, in his lucid times his faith remained firm.

He is widely known by the general public as an English poet and his collection of poems is still in print. Many of his poems are included in various collections.

He was given a home in the Vicarage of Olney in Buckinghamshire, by the converted Slave Trader, John Newton. There, for the congregation, he wrote hymns that still have a place in many church hymn books. The following Hymn tells of the Sovereign purposes of God in His providential care for His people, which is a remarkable testimony to Cowper's faith.

HYMN

God moves in a mysterious way
His wonders to perform;
He plants His footsteps in the sea,
And rides upon the storm.

Deep in unfathomable mines
Of never-failing skill
He treasures up His bright designs,
And works His sovereign will.

You fearful saints, fresh courage take,
The clouds you so much dread
Are big with mercy and shall break
In blessings on your head.

Judge not the Lord by feeble sense,
But trust Him for His grace,
Behind a frowning providence
He hides a smiling face.

His purposes will ripen fast,
Unfolding every hour,
The bud may have a bitter taste,
But sweet will be the flower.

Blind unbelief is sure to err.
And scan His work in vain,
God is His own interpreter
And He will make it plain.

Chapter 3

Pillar 2

The Gospel of Grace

There has been much confusion in past centuries and in the present day, concerning what the Gospel really is. The word 'gospel' is an old English word used to translate the meaning of the original Greek word which simply means 'Good News'. It refers to the good news of the coming of the Kingdom of God bringing salvation in Jesus Christ. What precisely is that 'Good News'?

The Apostle Paul gives us some important information about it in Galatians 1:6–9:

"I marvel that you are turning away so soon from Him who called you in the grace of Christ, **to a different gospel***, which is*

not another; but there are some who trouble you and want to **pervert the gospel** *of Christ. But even if we, or an angel from heaven, preach* **any other gospel** *to you than what we have preached to you, let him be accursed. As we have said before, so now I say again, if anyone preaches* **any other gospel** *to you than what you have received, let him be accursed." Galatians 1:6–9 NKJV*

Obviously, there were some who had strayed away from the original Gospel of Jesus Christ. They were trying to live by both systems...the system of the Old Covenant of the Law given by Moses...and the New Covenant of Grace which came by Jesus Christ.

This was causing confusion and keeping believers frustrated under a sense of condemnation.

The apostle is indicating that there should be no mixture of the Law of the Old Covenant and the New Covenant of Grace. It is ALL GRACE NOW!

Paul refers to the gospel as the "Gospel of Grace".

"But none of these things move me; nor do I count my life dear to myself, so that I may finish my race with joy, and the ministry

which I received from the Lord Jesus, to testify to the gospel of the grace of God."   Acts 20:24 NKJV

So what is "The Gospel of Grace"?

The Gospel of Grace can be expressed very simply by this statement…"Jesus Plus Nothing".

Jesus Christ the Son of God, became man and lived a life without sin. He came to make a "substitutionary atonement*" for all whom the Father had given Him, before the world began. He became sin on the cross for them, suffering and dying on the cross; as their substitute, paying the penalty for their sins, that they might become the righteousness of God in Him.

"For He made Him who knew no sin to be sin for us, that we might become the righteousness of God in Him."

2 Corinthians 5:21

(Read Romans Chapters 3 through 6, to see what this means.) All our sins (as believers) were reckoned to – or charged to His account (or imputed to) Him and His righteousness is reckoned (imputed) to us. Jesus became our **substitute** in His death and resurrection.

Are you noticing a pattern here? It is all about what Jesus has done for us. Our salvation is ALL of grace. Grace has been defined as the UNMERITED favour of God.

"For by grace you have been saved - through faith; and that not of yourselves, it is the gift of God. Not by (good) works that no one may boast." Ephesians 2:8,9

So the Gospel is the good news of God's grace to sinners through the shed blood of His Son on the cross. This is how it is a Gospel of Grace. Salvation is by grace through God-given faith in the atoning sacrifice of Christ ALONE.

Salvation is NOT a joint effort of God and us (Synergism*). It is **all** of God (Monergism*) who gets **all** the glory!

If Salvation depended in any way on us, then we would have a very shaky foundation. But since it is all of grace alone, through faith alone - in the finished work of Christ alone, it is a salvation that cannot be shaken. As the Hymn writer put it:

> "On Christ the solid rock I stand.
> All other ground is sinking sand.

The Gospel of Grace - declaring salvation by grace **alone** - is **the basis of the unity** we have as believers and as local churches, in Christ. There may be some differences of understanding of some teaching from the Bible on which we disagree,. For example, we may disagree on how a church should be governed. Or we may disagree on which spiritual gifts and ministries are available for all today. Or we may not agree on the details of Christ's coming again, etc. etc..

This should not be a cause of division. But clearly, from the apostle Paul's anathema (curse) of those who preach 'another gospel', this is not something we can ignore. If a gospel other than the gospel of grace is held to or preached, we must separate over it, because false 'gospels' bring spiritual death to hearers, not life.

. *"As we have said before, so now I say again, if anyone preaches **any other gospel** to you than what you have received, let him be accursed."* Galatians 1:9 NKJV

Augustus Montague Toplady

Another well-known Hymn was written by a young Minister of the Gospel – Augustus Montague Toplady, who lived from 1740 to 1778. He was minister of the little parish of Blagdon on the Mendip hills in Somerset. (England)

He was travelling one day through the gorge called Burrington Combe when a heavy rainstorm burst. He took shelter in a cleft in a great rock on the side of the gorge. The inspiration for the hymn came to him and he scribbled some thoughts in a small notebook. Later he wrote the hymn, likening his shelter in the rock to spiritual shelter in the riven (torn open) side of Christ the Rock of Ages.

The Hymn is full of teaching about our salvation by free and sovereign grace.

HYMN

Rock of Ages, cleft for me,
let me hide myself in Thee,
Let the water and the blood
From Thy riven side which flowed,
Be of sin the double cure,
Cleanse me from its guilt and power.

Not the labours of my hands
Can fulfil Thy law's demands;
Could my zeal no respite know,
Could my tears forever flow -
All for sin could not atone.
Thou must save and Thou alone.

Nothing in my hand I bring
Simply to Thy cross I cling,
Naked, come to Thee for dress,
Helpless look to Thee for grace,
Foul, I to the fountain fly,
Wash me, Saviour, or I die.

While I draw this fleeting breath,
When my eyelids close in death,
When I soar to realms unknown,
See Thee on Thy judgment throne,
Rock of Ages, cleft for me,
Let me hide myself in Thee.

Augustus Montague Tolplady 1772

Chapter 4

The Five Solas -

The Next Five Pillars

The Protestant Reformation of the 16th century changed Christianity forever. Roused to action by the corruption and abuses they saw in the Roman Catholic church of the time, pastors and leaders like Martin Luther and John Calvin spearheaded a movement that transformed Christianity and eventually led to the emergence of the Protestant churches that exist today.

The Reformers were guided by the conviction that the church of their day had drifted away from the essential, original teachings of Christianity, especially in regard to what it was taught about salvation—how people can be forgiven their sins through the death and resurrection of Jesus Christ and receive eternal life with God. This found expression particularly in the doctrine of "justification by faith alone". Martin Luther was challenged by the writings of the apostle Paul in his Letters to the Romans and the Galatians. For example:

"Therefore we conclude that a man is justified by faith apart from the deeds of the law." Romans 3:28

He discovered or rather, rediscovered the truth that we are ***justified*** - set right, or accounted righteous - before God, by faith and not by (good) works.

As we have said, the leaders of the Reformation sought to re-establish Christianity on the original message of Jesus and the teaching of the early church. But they were not as radical as some of those whom they called "Anabaptists' (Re-baptisers), especially about the nature of the church and who are the true members of the church. However, some teachings the Reformers rediscovered were clear and vital to the whole Reform movement. Central to the Bible truths they rediscovered were those which were later called **The Five 'Solas'.**

The Five Solas are five Latin phrases (or slogans) that emerged during that time and summarise the Reformers' convictions about the **essentials** of Christianity. The word **'Sola'** itself, is the Latin for **'Only'** or 'alone'.

The Five Solas are:

1. Sola Scriptura ("Scripture alone"): The Bible alone is our highest authority.

2. Sola Gratia ("Grace alone"): We are saved by the grace of God alone.

3. Sola Fide ("Faith alone"): We are saved through faith alone in Jesus Christ.

4. Solus Christus ("Christ alone"): Jesus Christ alone. His finished work on the cross alone is the ground of our salvation.

5. Soli Deo Gloria ("to the Glory of God alone"): All is for the glory of God and God alone.

Let's look at each of these five statements.

Chapter 5

Pillar 3

1. SOLA SCRIPTURA (The Scriptures alone)

Martin Luther publicly rebuked the Roman Catholic Church for its unbiblical teachings. The Roman Catholic Church threatened Luther with excommunication (and death) if he did not recant (reject – take back - his teachings). Martin Luther's reply was: "Unless therefore I am convinced by the testimony of Scripture, or by the clearest reasoning, unless I am persuaded by means of the passages I have quoted, and unless they thus render my conscience bound by the Word of God, I cannot and will not retract, for it is unsafe for a Christian to speak against his conscience. Here I stand, I can do no other; may God help me! Amen"

The Bible is the Word of God. For the Bible declares itself to be God-breathed, inerrant, and authoritative. (2 Timothy 3:16 Psalm 18:30 33:4 etc.) We also know that God does not change His mind or contradict Himself. (Malachi 3:6 etc.)

The Word of God therefore should be the **only** authority for the Christian faith. Traditions are valid only when they are based on Scripture and are in full agreement with Scripture. Traditions that contradict the Bible are not of God and are not a valid expression of the Christian faith.

The problem with the Roman Catholic Church, and many other churches, is that they base traditions on traditions which are based on traditions, often with the initial tradition not being in full harmony with the Scriptures. That is why Christians must always go back to *sola scriptura*, the authoritative Word of God, as the only solid basis for faith and practice.

In more recent centuries, various church groups (denominations) have adopted "Statements of Faith" which, it was assumed, were in accordance with the Scriptures. However, the **interpretation** of those Statements has frequently been regarded as more authoritative than the Scriptures themselves and have, in fact at times, been contrary to the teaching of the Scriptures. Giving primary importance to "Statements of Faith" has prevented those churches from being reformed or corrected by the teaching of the Scriptures.

So then, the first Sola, from which the other Solas are derived, states that the Scriptures are the single ultimate and trustworthy authority for faith and practice. This doesn't mean that the Bible is the only place where truth is found, but it does mean that everything else we learn about God and his world, and all other authorities, should be interpreted in the light of Scripture. The Bible gives us everything we need for our Christian doctrine..

2 Timothy 2:15 declares, *"Do your best to present yourself to God as one approved, a workman who does not need to be ashamed and who correctly handles the word of truth."*.

Every word of the 66 books of the Bible is infallibly* inspired by God's Holy Spirit. The Holy Spirit also helps us to understand, feed on and obey the Holy Scriptures.

The Bible and the Bible alone is the only rule given to direct us how to glorify God and to enjoy Him forever. No creed or council, no matter how ancient, can bind a believer's conscience. The Bible is God-breathed, written as holy men of old were moved by God.

"for prophecy never came by the will of man, but holy men of God spoke as they were moved by the Holy Spirit. " 2 Peter 1:21

We need no further revelation on God's thoughts about salvation, eternal life and godliness, than that which we have in the Bible. (See Hebrews 4:12,13) Believing in Sola Scriptura, we reject the need for so-called further revelations such as the Book of Mormon, the JW Watchtower, the supposed 'infallible' pronouncements of the Pope(s) and the traditions of men. Furthermore, we believe, the Holy Spirit will not declare anything that is **contrary** to the Bible. The Bible therefore must always hold the place of final authority in the lives of God's people.

While it is true that God has gifted some with a special ability to teach (Ephesians 4:11). no one believer knows and understands **all** that the Bible says. Yet, at the same time, its teachings for salvation and living the Christian life are plain. Nothing more is needed, nor are we dependent on any others for this. (1 John 2:27)

HYMN

How precious is the Book Divine,
By inspiration given!
Bright as a lamp its doctrines shine
To guide our souls to heaven
,
It's light, descending from above
Our gloomy world to cheer,
Displays a Saviour's boundless love
And brings His glories near,

It shows to man his wandering ways
And where his feet have trod,
And brings to view the matchless grace
Of a forgiving God,

When once it penetrates the mind
It conquers every sin,
The enlightened soul begins to find
The path of peace divine.

It sweetly cheers our drooping hearts
In this dark vale of tears,
Life, light, and joy it still imparts
And quells our rising fears.

This lamp through all the tedious night
Of life shall guide our way
Till we behold the clearer light
Of an eternal day,

John Fawcett 1740-1817

Chapter 6

Pillar 4

2. SOLA GRATIA (By Grace alone)

We are saved solely by God's grace and grace alone. **'Grace'** means 'the unmerited favour of God'. This indicates that salvation is entirely by the power and merciful kindness and goodness of God - **alone**.

We cannot earn our salvation by good works (good deeds). Nor by attempting to keep God's Law(s). Nor can we merit it by religious acts, such as attending church services or through the so-called 'sacraments'*.

Nor, as stated earlier, is salvation a combined effort where God does His part and we must do ours.

No human being **deserves** the favour of God. In our fallen sinful human nature not one of us was from the first, seeking for God or trying to understand Him. Because of our rebellion and sin we all deserve the punishment of hell. But grace intervened!

As the Hymn writer put it:

> "Grace first inscribed my name
> In God's eternal book,
> 'Twas grace that gave me to the Lamb,
> Who all my sorrows took."

We are saved entirely and only by **grace** alone. God's grace towards us is shown in the saving activity which was accomplished in the person of Christ Jesus. This saving work of Christ which took place in history, is the sole ground or basis for our acceptance by God both now and in eternity. Furthermore, every moment we live, we live by the good pleasure of the God of all grace. Although He is our creator He is not under any obligation to bless, help, save or do anything for any of us; however because of the new covenant in Christ and His character of Grace, His benefits and blessings flow to us in abundance! Although, *"all we like sheep have gone astray and have turned everyone to his own way, the LORD has laid on Him* (Jesus) *the iniquities of us all"*.(Isaiah 53:6) Now that is Grace!

We are saved because of a free gift which we do not deserve and have not earned. The gift of Christ's righteousness is free without a cost to us or finding a cause in us.

"For our sake he made him to be sin who knew no sin, so that in him we might become the righteousness of God." 2 Corinthians 5:21

This **substitution** has graciously been made by God for all who believe. Christ became sin (on the cross) so that we may become righteous – by the **gift** of righteousness.

Grace alone saves us apart from any human merit. The only contribution we make to Salvation is the sin from which we must be saved.

HYMN

O how the grace of God amazes me!
It loosed me from my bonds
And set me free.
What made it happen so?
'Twas His will, this much I know,
Set me, as now I show,
At liberty.

My God has chosen me,
Though one of nought,
To sit beside my King
In heaven's court.
Hear what my Lord has done!
O the love that made Him run
To meet His erring son!
This has God wrought.

Not for my righteousness,
For I have none,
But for His mercy's sake,
Jesus, God's Son,
Suffered on Calvary's tree -
Crucified with thieves was He.
Great was His grace to me,
His wayward one.

And when I think of how,
At Calvary,
He bore sin's penalty
Instead of me,
Amazed, I wonder why
He, the sinless One, should die

For one so vile as I,
My Saviour He!

Now all my heart's desire,
Is to abide
In Him, my Saviour dear,
In Him to hide;
My shield and buckler He,
Covering and protecting me,
From Satan's darts I'll be
Safe at His side.

Lord Jesus hear my prayer;
Your grace impart,
When evil thoughts arise
Through Satan's art,
O drive them far away
And, my God, from day to day,
Keep me beneath Your sway,
King of my heart!

Come now, the whole of me.
Eyes, ears and voice,
Join me creation all,
With joyful noise,
Praise Him who broke the chain
Holding me in sin's domain,
And set me free again!
Sing and rejoice!

E T Sibomana 1910-1975 Translated Rosemary Guillbrand 1915-2002

Chapter 7

Pillar 5

3. SOLA FIDE (Through Faith alone)

We are saved solely **through faith** in Jesus Christ because of God's grace and Christ's merit alone. We are not saved by our merits or declared righteous by our good works. God grants salvation not because of the good things we do, and despite our sin. (Which is why I keep on emphasising the fact!)

As humans, we inherited (from our ancestor Adam) a nature that is enslaved to sin. Because of our nature, we are naturally enemies of God and lovers of evil.

The Bible declares that we are (spiritually) dead in trespasses and sin. (Ephesians 2:1) Therefore we need to be made alive (regenerated – born again) first, before we can even begin to have faith in Christ. God graciously chooses to give us new hearts and new spirits so that we trust in Christ and are saved through faith alone. *"I will give you a new heart and put a new spirit in you; I will remove from you your heart of stone and give you a heart of flesh."* Ezekiel 36:26

God graciously preserves us and keeps us. *"*W*hen we are faithless toward him, he is still faithful. If we are faithless, He remains faithful; He cannot deny Himself."* 2 Timothy 2:13

We can only stand before God by His grace as He mercifully attributes to us the righteousness of Jesus Christ and attributes our sins to Him and the consequences of our sins. Jesus' life of perfect righteousness is counted as ours, and our sins and failure were counted to Jesus when He died on the cross.

"For He made Him who knew no sin to be sin for us, that we might become the righteousness of God in Him." 2 Corinthians 5:21

Sola fide and **sola gratia** together express the teaching of Ephesians 2:8-10

"For by grace you have been saved through faith. And this is not your own doing; it is the gift of God, not a result of works, so that no one may boast. For we are his workmanship, created in Christ Jesus for good works, which God prepared beforehand, that we should walk in them."

The Holy Spirit's gift of faith through the hearing of the gospel is **the sole means** by which Christ's substitutionary death is imputed (reckoned) to us for justification* unto life.

Faith alone enables us to embrace the free gift of righteousness which is in Christ alone. Faith does not **cause** God to save us. Faith, on the contrary, embraces the salvation which has already been accomplished by Christ's all sufficient sacrifice at the cross.

Faith takes hold of Christ Jesus as our only righteousness. Faith, therefore, is not a quality within us which God looks for in our hearts before he can pronounce us not guilty.

Faith, has never been and never will be the ground or cause of our salvation, rather, faith brings all that Christ accomplished as the Saviour, to his people and makes them His own.

Martin Luther's Contribution on "Faith Alone"

Luther came to understand that justification* (coming to be forever accounted perfectly righteous in God's sight) was **entirely** the work of God. This was clearly expressed in his book published in 1525 'On the Bondage of the Will' [4]. Luther based what he came to believe about predestination on Paul's Letter to the Ephesians and particularly on Ephesians 2:8–10. He wrote against the teaching of his day, which supposed that the righteous acts of believers are performed **in cooperation** with God. Luther wrote that Christians receive such righteousness entirely from outside themselves; that this righteousness not only comes from Christ but actually is the righteousness **of Christ**, imputed (reckoned) to believers.

"That is why faith alone makes a person just and fulfils the law. Faith is that which brings the Holy Spirit through the merits of Christ". Faith, for Luther, was a gift from God; the experience of being justified by faith was "as though I had been born again." His 'entry into Paradise', (as he felt it to be), was in this discovery about "the righteousness of God" – a discovery that "the just person" of whom the Bible speaks (as in Romans 1:17) lives by faith.

---

[4] 'On The Bondage of the Will" is still in print and well worth reading

HYMN

My faith has found a resting place,
From guilt my soul is freed,
I trust the ever-living One,
His wounds for me shall plead.

*I need no other argument,
I need no other plea,
It is enough that Jesus died,
And that He died for me.*

Enough for me that Jesus saves,
This ends my fear and doubt,
A sinful soul I come to Him,
He'll never cast me out.

My heart is leaning on the word,
The written word of God;
Salvation by my Saviour's Name,
Salvation through His blood.

My great physician heals the sick,
The lost He came to save;
For me His precious blood He shed,
For me His life He gave.

By Eliza Edmunds Hewitt 1851-1920

Chapter 8

Pillar 6

4. SOLUS CHRISTUS (In Christ alone)

God has given the ultimate revelation of himself to us by sending Jesus Christ, as we read in Colossians:

"He is the image of the invisible God, the firstborn over all creation. For by Him all things were created that are in heaven and that are on earth, visible and invisible, whether thrones or dominions or principalities or powers. All things were created through Him and for Him. And He is before all things, and in Him all things consist." Colossian 1:15-17

Only through God's gracious self-revelation in Jesus do we come to a saving and transforming knowledge of God.

Because God is holy and all humans are sinners (1 John 1:1 Hebrews 7:25 Romans 8:34), neither religious rituals nor good works can mediate between us and God. They cannot make us acceptable to God nor can they be the means by which we can be saved from the power and consequences of our sin.

"Nor is there salvation in any other, for there is no other name under heaven given among men by which we must be saved." other than the name of Jesus."   Acts 4:12

Salvation is in and through Christ alone. His sacrificial death alone can atone for sin.

Therefore He is also able to save to the uttermost those who come to God through Him, since He always lives to make intercession for them."   Hebrews 7:25

The Good News of salvation, calls upon all men everywhere, by God's grace, to repent and put their trust in the finished work of Christ alone for salvation from sin and death and hell. Nothing but the blood of Jesus will avail for this.

By 'the finished work' of Christ, we mean the completed work of salvation which he completely and fully accomplished by His sufferings and death on the cross.

Shortly before Jesus died on the cross, He called out, *"It is finished!"* (John 19:30) Indicating that the work of redemption* had now been completed.

The heart of the gospel is not about us. The heart of the gospel is Christ *for us*. This was the essence of the apostle Paul's message: that Christ came for us, to do *for us* what we ourselves could not and would not do. He came and lived a life in human form without sin. He was crucified. He was raised from death. He ascended to heaven. He will return again in glory. . The good news is that we have no part in this story. Believers are the recipients. We're beggars; we're not contributors to the story of Redemption."

CHRIST IS ALL AND IN ALL
(Colossians 3:11)

1) IN CHRIST WE HAVE REDEMPTION, THE FORGIVENESS OF ALL OUR SINS.

Colossians 1:14: *"in whom we have redemption, the forgiveness of sins."* Colossians 2:13: *"When you were dead in your transgressions and the uncircumcision of your flesh, He made you alive together with Him, having forgiven us all our transgressions."* Christ is the answer to the problem of guilt! If Christ is **all** in the sense of forgiving us **all** our transgressions; you can't add anything of your own to what He supplies.

The Puritan Jeremiah Burroughs put it like this:

"As far as God sees Christ in anyone, He accepts them. If Christ is not there, no matter what they have, He does not regard them."

To be right with God, you can't come through religion or rituals or race or moral improvement – attempting to live a good life. You can only come through Jesus Christ and Him crucified. Make sure that you are **in Him** through faith in His shed blood alone!

2) IN CHRIST WE ARE COMPLETE.

Paul states (Colossians 2:10), *"In Him you have been made complete."* But in Colossians 1:28, he also says that his aim is to *"present every man complete in Christ."* This is the tension that we often find in Paul's writings, between the righteousness which God imputes (reckons) to us and what we must strive to become practically, to walk with Him in holiness of life.

We have **all** spiritual blessings in Christ (Eph. 1:3), but it takes all of life and all of eternity to discover fully what those blessings are (Eph. 2:7). But the point is, if you have Christ in you,, then you are you **complete in Him**.

3) IN CHRIST, WE HAVE ALL THE TREASURES OF WISDOM AND KNOWLEDGE.

Colossians 2:3: *"in whom are hidden all the treasures of wisdom and knowledge."* "Hidden treasures" implies that we need to dig and seek out these riches. They aren't all just lying around on the surface. These are treasures which are more in value than the wisdom and knowledge of this world.

4) IN CHRIST, WE HAVE THE HOPE OF ETERNAL GLORY.

Colossians 1:27: *"to whom* [the saints] *God willed to make known what is the riches of the glory of this mystery among the Gentiles, which is Christ in you, the hope of glory."* Colossians 3:4: *"When Christ, who is our life, is revealed, then you also will be revealed with Him in glory."*

If that is your eternal destiny, then, by God's grace, Christ will become your hope in every trial and difficulty of this life. We can have His comfort in our trials, knowing that they are nothing compared to the *"eternal weight of glory"* (2 Cor. 4:17) that awaits us with Him throughout the ages.

Christ is all, in God's eternal purpose, and all in God's plan of salvation.

So salvation is **'Solus Christus"** – in and through and by Christ **alone.**

HYMN

Immortal honours rest on Jesus' head,
My God, my portion and my living bread;
In Him I live, upon Him cast my care,
He saves from death, destruction and despair.

He is my refuge in each deep distress,
The Lord my strength and glorious righteousness.
Through floods and flames He leads me safely on,
And daily makes His sovereign goodness known.

My every need He richly will supply,
Nor will His mercy ever let me die;
In Him there dwells a treasure all divine,
And matchless grace has made that treasure mine.

O that my soul could love and praise `Him more,
His beauties trace, His majesty adore,
Live near His heart, upon His bosom lean.
Obey His voice and all His will esteem.

By William Gadsby 1773 - 1844

Chapter 9

Pillar 7

5. SOLI DEO GLORIA (To the Glory of God alone)

Some who are new to or ignorant of the Christian faith, find it odd that God should want **all glory** to be given to Him. This is because they are comparing God to men who are full of self-importance, seeking the adulation of all around them.

But God is totally different in that all glory not only is His by right, but if any glory is given to another, then He is being robbed. This could be seen as an attempt, if it were possible, to take away from His divine nature. He would then be regarded as someone less than the **only** God, the God of all creation.

Glory belongs to God alone. God's glory is the central motivation for creation and for the salvation of His elect. It is not for improving the world, or the lives of people generally in the world — though that may be a wonderful by-product. God is not a means to an end — he is both the means and the end.

The purpose and goal of all of life is to give glory to God alone:

"Whether you eat or drink, or whatever you do, do all to the glory of God.".   1 Corinthians 10:31.

As The Westminster Catechism puts it, the chief end (purpose) of man (human life) is "to glorify God and enjoy him forever."

The Lord Jesus is the visible manifestation of the invisible God. He is God manifest in the flesh and it is in Christ alone that God has fully declared Himself. Christ is the only way to the Father, the only Door to heaven, our only mediator, advocate and High Priest. His doing and dying on our behalf is the sole basis of our acceptance and continued fellowship with God.

"Jesus said to him, "I am the way, the truth, and the life. No one comes to the Father except through Me."   John 14:6

Christ alone is our righteousness and true salvation comes by being found in Christ alone.

God has saved us for His glory! We who are now justified are called to glory in the cross of Christ and to make His person and saving works the central declaration of our Christian witness. Our lives are to be lived to the glory of God alone. We are to *"Give unto the LORD the glory due unto his name;"* Psalm 29:2.

Christ has died and risen again. Through His death on the cross we who believe, were purchased by His precious blood; given the earnest* (down- payment) of the Spirit and sealed (so as to be kept) by that same Holy Spirit. If we have received such grace, our response will be to want to glorify God!

Salvation is in accordance with Scriptures alone, by grace alone, through faith alone in the finished work of Christ alone and all to the glory of God alone."

This sums up the "Five Solas" – a statement worth memorising!

HYMN

Glory, glory everlasting
Be to Him who bore the cross!
Who redeemed our souls by tasting
Death, the death deserved by us.
Spread His glory,
Who redeemed His people thus.

His is love, 'tis love unbounded,
Without measure, without end;
Human thought is here confounded,
Praise the Saviour!
Magnify the sinner's friend.

While we hear the wondrous story
Of the Saviour's cross and shame ,
Sing we 'Everlasting glory
Be to God, and to the Lamb!
Saints and angels,
Glory give to His great Name!

By Thomas Kelly 1769-1855

This concludes seven of the Pillars:

The Sovereignty of God.
The Gospel of Grace.
The Five Solas..

We turn next to the final **five Pillars** that make up the twelve:

The Five Doctrines of Grace.

Chapter 10

The Doctrines of Grace
Introduction

Over a period of about 350 years, and especially in the past 75 years, evangelical Christianity has been seriously undermined by doctrines which have come from the teaching of a Minister of the Dutch Reformed Church, called Jacobus Arminius. He lived from 1580 to 1609.

Some Church groups (Denominations), following the Reformers, have, in the course of history, produced various "Reformation **Statements of Faith**". These have been attempts to define what each church group believed were important doctrines. For example, The Westminster Confession, The Longer and Shorter Westminster Catechisms, The 39 Articles of the Church of England, The First London

Baptist Confession of Faith 1644/46, The (Second) Baptist Confession of Faith 1689, The Heidelberg Catechism, etc...

Those holding to these Statements of Faith, all firmly reject this set of teachings by Arminius, which is usually referred to as 'Arminian" or "Arminianism".

HOW DID THE ARMINIAN VIEW COME ABOUT?

At the beginning of the Reformation, the truths of God's Word were revealed afresh to Wycliffe and Tyndale, who were among the first to produce a version of the Scriptures in English. Martin Luther in Germany came to realise the truth of "justification by faith ALONE." Good works could not, of themselves save any man. All the great Reformers were united in the central truth of the Gospel - that salvation was by GRACE ALONE, through FAITH ALONE in the finished work of CHRIST ALONE. It was the French reformer John Calvin who came to see that the doctrine of the Sovereignty of God was also of the greatest importance in our understanding of all the other teaching of the Bible.

Jacob Hermann (known by his Latin name - Jacobus Arminius). Began to teach a 'new' doctrine. According to Arminius, God's "predestination" of individuals is based upon His foreknowledge of whether each human being will freely chose to accept or reject Christ. This was not altogether a new doctrine. It was a form of "Pelagianism" - a heresy taught by a monk called Pelagius back in the 4th Century. (His teaching was opposed by the very influential Church leader and teacher - Augustine, known by many as Saint Augustine, Bishop of Hippo.)

A few years after the death of Arminius, the Protestant Churches on the Continent and also here in England and Scotland, were so concerned about the spread of his teaching, that an international Conference of Ministers was called and met at Dort in the Netherlands in 1618 at what came to be known as **The Synod of Dort.** The result of their deliberations was that they identified the FIVE POINTS OF ARMINIANISM. They found these 5 Points to be contrary to the teaching of the Bible.

Briefly, those Five Points were:

1. All men have sufficient grace remaining in their fallen state so that they can, if they choose, exercise faith toward God.

2. Their free choice to believe in God is the reason why God in turn, choses them as His elect, granting them forgiveness and eternal life.

3. Jesus died for all men inclusively. He loves all men equally.

4. All men have free will and can choose to believe in God or refuse His grace.

5. True believers can at any point turn away from God and be lost . Their salvation depends on their continuing perseverance.

The Synod of Dort

To correct this teaching the Synod of Dort restated Five DOCTRINES OF GRACE, which because Calvin had, to some extent, taught them some 50 years before, came later also to be (wrongly) known as The Five Points of Calvinism. (John Calvin's teaching covered much more than this. These five Points do not define all that Calvin taught [5].)

These five points are also known as the **TULIP** doctrines - the initial letters of which stand for:

Total depravity, Unmerited election, Limited atonement, Irresistible grace, and Perseverance of the saints.

---

[5] See Calvin's "Institutes of the Christian Faith"

These doctrines have been consistently held by evangelical churches of every age. They were clearly taught by Augustine in the Fifth Century, by Luther, Calvin, Cranmer, George Whitfield, William Carey, Charles Spurgeon, Bishop Ryle etc. and by all the leading Puritans and by those who today are referred to as "Reformed".

A modified form of Arminianism was held by John Wesley, (he did not believe in Limited Atonement and believed it possible for true believers to lose their salvation), and through his (Arminian Methodist and perfectionist) teaching, and also through the later influence of "theological liberals", Arminianism spread through the Methodist and 'Brethren' movements and has become so widespread that today, many of those who regard themselves as true "Bible-believing Christians" have come to assume that this (false) doctrine is normal and biblical.

A careful and prayerful study of all the texts quoted here, read in their contexts, will demonstrate the truths of **The Doctrines of Grace** which point to the one true Gospel - the Gospel of Grace, that gives ALL the glory to God.

A Note About John Calvin and the Doctrines of Grace

It is unfortunate that many who hold to the Five Doctrines of Grace are at times referred to as "Calvinists". There are those who regard themselves as "Reformed", who are quite happy to be called "Calvinists".

But simply because someone holds to the Doctrines of Grace, (and Calvin was not himself **totally** in agreement with them), it does not mean that he or she believes or holds to all that Calvin taught.

Calvin was, without doubt, an outstanding leader of the Reformation, but he was a man of his time and he taught some things that were still a 'hangover' from his previous Roman Catholic beliefs.

However, he was very clear on the Sovereignty of God and the Gospel of Grace. But The Synod of Dort , which restated the Five Doctrines, did not take place until 40 years after Calvin's death.

HYMN

Grace has a thrilling sound
To each believer's ear;
That peace with God through Christ is found
Is news I gladly hear.

Grace first inscribed my name
In God's eternal book,
And grace has brought me to the Lamb,
Who all my sorrows took.

Grace led my wandering feet
To tread the heavenly road,
And grace supplies each hour
I meet while pressing on to God.

Grace taught my soul to pray
And made my eyes o'erflow;
His grace has kept me to this day
And will not let me go.

Grace all our work shall crown
Through everlasting days;
The heavenly home God gives his own
Shall echo with our praise.

Philip Doddridge 1702-1751 (Slightly modernised)

Chapter 11

Pillar 8

The First Doctrine of Grace

"Total Depravity"

Man's depravity, as a result of the Fall, is total. That is to say, sin has corrupted him in every aspect of his being. That does not mean he is utterly evil in every way - as the Devil is - but that he is **affected by evil in every way**. He does not possess free will – by nature he is free only to sin - because he is bound to Satan who takes man captive at his will. All men are born into this world spiritually dead in trespasses and sins so that their souls are irresistibly drawn to, and blinded by, the god of this world. Man is depraved in the sense that he is spiritually dead, blind, deaf, and unteachable in the things of

God. Whether he realises it or not, He is ruled by Satan through his perverse heart and corrupt soul. His thinking, emotions, will, and physical desires have all been perverted and corrupted.

All are totally affected by sin:

Rom 5:12 '..... *just as through one man sin entered the world, and death through sin, and thus death spread to all men, because all sinned...]*

. Jer.17:9 *"The heart is deceitful above all things, and desperately wicked; who can know it?*

See Rom.3:9-12 Psalm 14:1-3 Psalm 58:1-3 Prov.20:9.

All are born spiritually dead:

Eph.5:8 *For you were once darkness, but now you are light in the Lord...* Col 2:13 *And you, being dead in your sins... hath he made alive* ... Eph.2:1 *And you has he made alive, who were dead in trespasses and sins..* Eph.2:5 *Even when we were dead in sins, he made us alive together with Christ, (by grace you are saved);* 1 John 5:12 *He that has the Son has life; and he who does not have the Son of God does not have life.*

See also Psalm 58:3 Psalm 51:5 John 3:3 Gen. 8:21.

Taken Captive at Satan's Will: 2 Tim 2:25,26 *"In meekness instructing those that oppose themselves; if God perhaps will give them repentance to the acknowledging of the truth;*

And that they may recover themselves out of the snare of the devil, who are taken captive by him at his will."

"You are of your father the devil, and the lusts of your father you will do." John 8;44

In their natural state, all are irresistibly drawn to Satan:

Eph.2:2,3. *Wherein in time past you walked according to the course of this world, according to the prince of the power of the air, the spirit that now works in the children of disobedience: Among whom also we all had our way of life in times past in the lusts of our flesh, fulfilling the desires of the flesh and of the mind; and were by nature the children of wrath, even as others.*

John 3:19 *And this is the condemnation, that light is come into the world, and men loved darkness rather than light, because their deeds were evil.*

The natural man is spiritually unteachable:

1 Cor. 2:14 *The natural man receives not the things of the Spirit of God: for they are foolishness to him: neither can he know them, because they are spiritually discerned.*

You may be asking, "How does this teaching square with the thought that there are good people in the world as well as evil? For example, I happen to have some very kind neighbours, who are not believers.

The brief answer concerns their motivation. "WHY are they kind to you? Does it spring from self regard or self pride? Are they kind because they want to think well of themselves? Would they act differently if you were very rude to them or damaged their property?

Self esteem is highly regarded in society and pride is perceived as a virtue,. But God sees it as the sin of idolatry, in the worship of self!

HYMN

Not what these hands have done
Can save this guilty soul,
Not what this toiling flesh has borne
Can make my spirit whole.

Not what I feel or do
Can give me peace with God;
Not all my prayers , and sighs, and tears
Can bear my awful load.

Thy work alone, O Christ,
Can ease this weight of sin,
Thy blood alone, O Lamb of God,
Can give me peace within.

Thy love to me ,O God,
Not mine, O Lord to Thee,
Can rid me of this dark unrest,
And set my spirit free.

Thy grace, alone, O God.
To me can pardon speak,
Thy power alone, O Son of God,
Can this sore bondage break.

I bless the Christ of God,
I rest on love divine,
And with unfaltering lip and heart,
I call this Saviour mine.

By Horatius Bonar 1808-1889

Chapter 12

Pillar 9

The Second Doctrine of Grace

"Unconditional Election"

(Or "Unmerited Election")

Election to salvation is grounded entirely in the free and sovereign will of God and in His purpose for those whom he chose "in Christ Jesus" before the foundation of the world.

God's foreknowledge is based upon His purpose and His purpose is the manifestation of His sovereign will. Since man is incapable of giving himself life, opening his own blind eyes, or teaching himself spiritual truth, God must choose to act on man's behalf.

The work of Regeneration (new birth/giving new life), therefore must come about **before** faith and repentance can be expressed. God must first "open the heart" and cause His elect "to will and to do" that which is pleasing to Him. Otherwise no one would believe, for no one would, nor indeed could, choose to believe.

Far from being the puppets of God - men are **set free to choose God** and His will, by sovereign grace alone. Until men receive that grace, they remain the slaves of sin.

God Chooses, Not Man:

John 15:16 *You have not chosen me, but I have chosen you....*
Acts 13:48 *... as many as were ordained to eternal life believed.*

Phil 2:13 *For it is God who works in you both to will and to do of his good pleasure.*

Election Based On God's Purpose (Plan):

Eph 1:11 *.... being predestined according to the purpose of him who works all things after the counsel of his own will:*

2 Tim 1:9 *Who has saved us, and called us with a holy calling, not according to our works, but according to his own purpose and grace, which was given us in Christ Jesus before the world began,*

Rom. 8:28 *And we know that all things work together for good to those who love God, to those who are the called according to his purpose.*

Man is Incapable - God Must Initiate:

John 6:44 *No man can come to me, except the Father who has sent me draw him: and I will raise him up at the last day.*

Matt.11:27 *... no man knows the Son, but the Father; neither knows any man the Father, save the Son, and he to whoever the Son will reveal him.*

Acts 16:14 *....Lydia...heard us: whose heart the Lord opened, that she attended to the things that were spoken by Paul.*

See also Heb.12:2 Luke 17:5 etc. etc.

Begotten of God:

1 Pet 1:3 *Blessed be the God and Father of our Lord Jesus Christ, which according to his abundant mercy has begotten us again*

unto a living hope by the resurrection of Jesus Christ from the dead…

God chose to save certain sinners, not for anything good He saw in them, but simply and freely of His own love and GRACE. Otherwise Grace is not Grace, for "Grace" by definition is the UMERITED favour of God.

Notice carefully the following statement: "God's sovereign will is manifested in sovereign grace and all to His own glory."

If God were to choose you or me for salvation because He saw something particularly good in us, or in response to something good He **foresaw** that we would do, to merit His love – then it would not be **totally of grace** on His part and therefore He would not have ALL the glory.

One day, I was walking on the shingle beach near my home. It stretches for miles along Lyme Bay, called "Chesil Beach". It is composed of millions and millions of pebbles worn smooth by the sea. I was thinking about 'Unmerited Election' and how to illustrate it in my next sermon.

Around me, at my feet were a countless number of small pebbles. I reached down and chose one. I purposely did not choose it because of its appearance or size. I simply chose it because I wanted to chose it! I put it in my pocket and have kept it ever since.

Now I realise that my choice was not **entirely** of my own supposed 'free will'. It was conditioned by all kinds of factors. For example, the spot on which I was standing; the day and time I happened to be there on the beach; that there were millions of pebbles there to choose from as well, etc. etc.

But God, unlike me or you, is not bound by anything other than His own character and attributes. (For example, God cannot tell a lie). So it is that He has freely chosen a particular number from among mankind for salvation. That choice was not conditioned on anything other than His sovereign will which is in accord with His holy character and divine attributes.

This choice of God is for few rather than many from the whole of mankind (Matthew 7:14). But nevertheless, we are told that it is still "a multitude which no man can number". Read this quote from the Book of Revelation:

And they sang a new song, saying:
"You are worthy to take the scroll'
And to open its seals; For You were slain,
And have redeemed us to God by Your blood

Out of every tribe and tongue and people and nation.
And have made us kings and priests to our God;
And we shall reign on the earth."

Then I looked, and I heard the voice of many angels around the throne, the living creatures, and the elders; and the number of them was ten thousand times ten thousand, and thousands of thousands, saying with a loud voice:

"Worthy is the Lamb who was slain
To receive power and riches and wisdom,
And strength and honour and glory and blessing!"

And every creature which is in heaven and on the earth and under the earth and such as are in the sea, and all that are in them, I heard saying:

"Blessing and honour and glory and power
Be to Him who sits on the throne,
And to the Lamb, forever and ever!"
      Revelation 5:9-13

HYMN

From whence this fear and unbelief?
Has not the Father put to grief
His spotless Son for us?
And will the righteous Judge of men
Condemn me for that debt of sin
Which Lord, was charged on Thee?
Now cancelled at the cross?

Complete atonement Thou hast made
And to the utmost limit paid
All that Thy people owed.
Nor will God's wrath my soul distress,
If sheltered in Thy righteousness
And covered by Thy blood.

If Christ my discharge hath procured
And freely in my place endured
The whole of wrath divine –
God will not payment twice demand
First at my dying Saviour's hand,
And then again at mine.

Turn then my soul to joy and rest
,The merits of my great High Priest
Have bought my liberty.
Trust in His all-sufficient blood,
Ending my banishment from God,
For Jesus died for me!

by Augustus Montague Toplady (1740-1778)

Chapter 13

Pillar 10

The Third Doctrine of Grace

"Limited Atonement"

(Or "Effective Atonement")

Atonement has been made for the elect only, since Christ died only for those whom the Father gave Him to be His Bride. Only the saints or elect ones are ever said to be "beloved of God", for they alone are the objects of His saving grace. (Some describe this as "Limited" atonement, because it is limited to the elect only; hence the L in TULIP.) If Christ died for all men

inclusively, then absolutely all will be saved. But God cannot be a just God and punish twice for the same sins. If Christ bore the sins of all men inclusively, then God could not punish any, nor send any man to hell.

The truth is, Christ bore the sins of **many**. He died for His sheep - and not for the goats. His Name was called Jesus because he would save HIS PEOPLE from their sins. (Matthew 1:21) He died for all, in the sense that he died for all his people which are drawn from all KINDS of men, in all nations and down through all the ages, not merely from among the Jews.

It is obvious from the fact that many have already gone, and many may yet go, to a lost eternity, that Christ's blood was shed only for the elect who are saved by His unmerited favour. If Christ died to atone for all men inclusively, then He obviously failed! But when He cried out from the Cross, *"It is finished!"* - then a finished work of redemption had been completed. He accomplished an effective atonement for all those whom the Father had given Him from the whole world - from every tribe, language and nation. His victory was demonstrated in the resurrection.

John 10:14,15 *I am the good shepherd, and know **my sheep**, and am known of mine...and I lay down my life for **the sheep**.* Rom. 5:8 *But God commends his love toward **US**, in that, while we were yet sinners, Christ died **for US**.* Gal 1:3,4 (Note the emphasis).

*Grace be to you and peace from God the Father, and from our Lord Jesus Christ, Who gave himself for **OUR** sins, that he might deliver US from this present evil world, according to THE WILL OF GOD and **OUR** Father:* Rom. 8:32,33 *He that spared not his own Son, but delivered him up **for US** all, how shall he not with him also freely give **US** all things? Who shall lay any thing to the charge of God's **ELECT**?* Eph.5:25 *... as Christ also loved the **CHURCH**, and gave himself for it;* (added emphasis)

Shortly before Jesus went to the cross He prayed: *"I pray for them: **I pray not for the world**, but for those who You have given me; for they are Yours."* John 17:9

Col 1:12 - 21 *Giving thanks unto the Father, which hath made **us** meet to be partakers of the inheritance of the saints in light: Who hath delivered **US** from the power of darkness, and hath translated **US** into the kingdom of his dear Son: In whom we have redemption through his blood, even the forgiveness of sins*

...21. And you, that were sometime alienated and enemies in your mind by wicked works, yet now hath he reconciled.

1 Thessalonians 1:4 *Knowing, brethren beloved, your* **ELECTION** *of God.* (added emphasis).

Colossians 3:12 *Put on therefore, as THE ELECT of God, holy and beloved, bowels of mercies, kindness, humbleness of mind, meekness, long-suffering;* (The word "Church" means "Elect-assembly" - chosen/called-out-group "**ecclesia**" Greek).

"Free Will " or "Accountability"?

Careful study of the texts above will show that they do not support the idea of "free will", but they deal with Man's responsibility towards God and his accountability if he does not obey God. There are NO Scriptures which teach that man has a "free will" - the phrase does not occur anywhere in the Bible. Arminius reasoned (contrary to the Scripture) that "God has no right to hold a man accountable to believe, or to condemn him for unbelief, if man's will is not free to do so."

This is like saying a man driven by lust should not be held responsible for rape or child-molesting, nor punished for it, because he cannot control himself. (Or that a slug is not responsible for eating my lettuces because it is a slug.)

There may be different degrees of judicial (legal) or moral accountability according to knowledge etc. but as a creature created by God, all men are responsible for all their thoughts and actions. God says *"Every one of us shall give account", and those who reject His Word will be punished in the Lake of Fire.*

The Scriptures teach that there is sufficient light given to all men inclusively that, should any have the slightest inclination to come to the Light, they will be saved. The fact is that man is so affected by sin (his total depravity) that he loves darkness and hates the light and will not come to it of himself.

See: John 1:9 3:19 Rom. 1:18-20 Man is responsible to obey the Word of God and accountable when he refuses.

Particular Redemption

This doctrine is sometimes referred to as "Particular Redemption". This refers to the fact that God has chosen **particular** individuals for salvation from among mankind. It was for these that the Son of God came from heaven to earth, in order to to redeem* them through His death on the cross.

You may have heard of "Strict and Particular Baptist Churches". This simply means that they are 'Strict' as to who can or should partake of the Lord's Supper; and 'Particular" means that they hold to the doctrine of **Particular** Redemption, as distinct from 'General Baptists' who hold to 'General Redemption'; general meaning the opposite of particular.

Provided we understand how the word 'particular' is being used, **'Particular Redemption'** might be a better title for this third Doctrine of Grace. This is because when it is referred to as 'Limited' Atonement, it may be misunderstood as limiting the power and scope of Christ's ability to save.

There may be lingering thoughts in your mind questioning the reason why God chose to save only a portion of mankind. If so, then we suggest you might give some careful thought to Chapter 9 of Paul's letter to the Romans where this issue is raised.

HYMN

O what matchless condescension
The eternal God displays,
Claiming our supreme attention
To His boundless works and ways;
His own glory
He reveals in gospel days.

In the person of the Saviour
All His majesty is seen,
Love and justice shine forever;
And without a veil between,
We approach Him,
And rejoice in His dear name.

Would we view His highest glory,
Here it shines in Jesus' face;
Sing and tell the pleasing story,
O you sinners saved by grace.
And with pleasure
Bid the guilty Him embrace.

In His highest work redemption,
See His glory in a blaze;
Beyond mortal comprehension,
Higher than an angel's praise,
Grace and justice
Here unite in endless praise.

True, 'tis sweet and solemn pleasure,
God to view in Christ the Lord;
Here He smiles, and smiles forever;
May my soul His name record,
Praise and bless Him,
And His wonders spread abroad.

By William Gadsby 1773-1844

Chapter 14

Pillar 11

The Fourth Doctrine of Grace

"Invincible Grace"

This Doctrine is also referred to as "Irresistible Grace"

Since it is the decreed [6] will of God that those whom He gave to His dear Son in eternity past should be saved, He will surely act in sovereign grace in such a way that the elect will find the call of Christ irresistible. This does not mean that God forces

---

[6] By 'decreed' will, we refer to that aspect of God's will that is commanded or effected in such a way that it cannot be resisted or reversed.

the elect to trust in His Son but rather, that He gives them life and that life puts the desire in their hearts, and sets them free to repent of their sins and to put their trust wholly in Him for salvation. The spiritually dead human soul finds the spirit of Satan irresistible, but the living (born-again) human spirit finds the God of the living irresistible in bringing them to saving faith..

Regeneration (giving new spiritual life) is the work of God and must first be brought about through the Holy Spirit before there can be repentance and faith. It cannot be the **result** of repentance and faith.

Paul the apostle, first known as Saul, is a clear example of "invincible grace". In Acts 9 at the very moment when he was the leading figure in the persecution and killing of believers and in strong-willed rebellion against God and His Christ, he was converted.

GOD'S DECREED WILL IS IRRESISTIBLE

Men and women speak of "falling in love". This is where one person is drawn strongly in affection to another. This is not perceived so much as a matter of choice, but rather of **a response.** If you have ever 'fallen in love", you will readily identify the experience! The way in which the Father draws sinners to Christ by the Holy Spirit, is such that they will find it an irresistible response, rather than an active choice. Yet, as with "falling in love", it results in an active choice!

Dan.4:35 *He (God) does according to His will in the army of heaven and among all the inhabitants of the earth. No one can restrain His hand or say to Him, "What have You done?"*

Isaiah 46: 9,10 *"...I am God, and there is no other; I am God and there is none like Me, declaring the end from the beginning, and from ancient times things that are not yet done, saying, "My counsel shall stand, And I will do all my pleasure."*

John 6:44 *No one can come to Me unless the Father who sent Me draws him;*

GOD WILLS (DECREES) THE SALVATION OF THE ELECT

John 6:37 *"All that the Father gives Me, shall come to Me!"*

John 6:29 *"This is the work of God, that you believe on Him who He has sent."*

THE FATHER BEGETS THOSE HE HAS WILLED

James 1:18 *"Of His own will He begat US....."* John 1:13 *"Who were born, not of blood, nor of the will of the flesh, not of the will of man, but (who were born) of God."*

ACCOMPLISHED BY GOD GIVING LIFE

John 5:21 *"The Son gives life to whom He will."* Ephes. 2:4,5 *"God who is rich in mercy, for His great love with which he loved US, even when we were dead in sins, made US alive with Christ (by grace you are saved)."*

Acts 11:18 *"Then God has also granted repentance unto life to the Gentiles."*

EFFECTUALLY APPLIED BY THE HOLY SPIRIT

Titus 3:5 *"He saved us (not by works of righteousness which we have done, but according to His mercy), by the washing of regeneration and renewing of the Holy Spirit."*

SO WHY WITNESS? WHY BE HOLY?

SOME WHO HOLD TO THE TEACHING OF ARMINIUS accuse those who hold to the Bible Doctrines of Grace of a form of 'fatalism'. They do so because they perceive that belief in irresistible grace and the sovereignty of God in saving sinners and in keeping them unto eternal life leaves no possibility of choice. So it appears to make men robots or puppets..

"Why bother to witness?" they ask. "If God is going to save men anyway, why bother to strive to live a holy life, if there is no possibility of believers being lost in the end?" (To quote a phrase "Once saved - always saved").

The Scriptural answers are clear and simple. We witness because God has commanded us: *"You shall be my witnesses..."* We witness to the Person and Work of Christ because it is by the *"foolishness of preaching"* that God is pleased to saved those who believe. If it were left to a supposed 'free will' on man's part, then none would be saved, for no one has a will that is free from sin and the power of Satan.

We witness because we are *"labourers together with God."* (1 Cor:3.9) The truth is that God is Sovereign in the MEANS of Salvation as well as in the ENDS. He makes His people willing in the day of His power. (see Psalm 110:3)

As to the keeping power of God - "those who are born of God do not continue in sin." (See 1 John 3:8,9) - Believers can and do fall into sin, but because of the seed (of new life) within them, they will not continue in sin and be lost. This is the clear teaching of John. Hebrews 6:4 –8 refers to those who have "tasted" - not those who have been fed, and continue to be fed. See 2 Peter 1:4,5 and Jude verse 24.

WHO ACTS FIRST?

As we have already indicated, those who follow the teaching of Arminius believe that the human will is one of the **causes** of regeneration (This is an expression of the old heresy of synergism*). They believe that election is based on the foreknowledge of God who foresaw "those who would believe" back in eternity past. Foreknowing those who would freely will to repent of their sins and make a decision to place their faith in Christ, God then elected them to salvation. This means that repentance and faith are man's "good works" whereby he establishes the condition for his being chosen to be saved. Arminianism therefore is a "works religion" to the extent that man must accomplish the good works of repentance and faith, with only the 'general aid' of the Holy Spirit, who according to Arminius is given to all men alike.

The great Reformers taught that God **alone** is the CAUSE of regeneration. Knowing that no man can or will establish any condition which can serve as a basis for his election, they follow the Scriptural position which declares that "foreknowledge" is grounded in the "purpose" of God to elect some to salvation without good works on their part. (By sovereign grace - unmerited favour -alone!)

Every work that is related to salvation is God's work, for He alone can regenerate, give life to the dead, open blind eyes, unstop deaf ears, evoke faith in Jesus Christ, illumine the dark recesses of man's evil heart of unbelief, and grant true repentance of sins by establishing a desire for purity in doctrine and life. The true saving faith is *"not of works, lest any man should boast"* (Ephes.2:8,9), because it insists on giving God **all** the glory for all that is good.

Who is "Irresistible" and Why

One of the ideas so prevalent among Arminian "evangelicals" is that the lost are longing to hear the Gospel and hungry for the things of God! Our Lord is very clear in His teaching that the world hates Him, hates His Word, and hates His messengers. (See John 15:15 and following.) Innate (inborn, inbred) sin is the reason for the world hating God and His elect. Satan is the god of all dead spirits, angelic and human. The spirits of men who are born into this world 'dead in trespasses and sin' are irresistibly drawn to the leader of the spiritually dead. This is why no unregenerate person ever freely 'wills' to turn to God. How can a dead man do anything of his own will? By nature all men are not only 'dead' to God, but paradoxically the Scripture also declares that they are at enmity with God - they are not drawn to Him, but repelled by Him. Gen. 3:15 Rom. 8:7

However, for the same reason all living spirits find the God of the living "irresistible". They cannot help being drawn to Him, trusting Him, loving Him, just as before they were born-again by the Spirit of God, they were drawn to Satan, trusting the Lie,

John 1:13 *"Who were born (1) not of blood, (2) nor of the will of the flesh, (3) nor of the will of man, but of God.*

John 1:12 must be linked with John 1:13 to be understood. Those who have the right to be God's children are the ones who have received the free unmerited gift of Christ as their Saviour and Lord..

So whose "will" determines the conception and birth of the one who is born again? It is the will of the Father in heaven!

Salvation is of the Lord! Jonah 2:9

HYMN

All that I was, my sin, my guilt.
My death, was all my own;
All that I am I owe to Thee,
My gracious God, alone.

The evil of my former state
Was mine, and only mine,
The good in which I now rejoice,
Is Thine, and only Thine.

The darkness of my former state,
The bondage – all was mine,
The light of life in which I walk,
The liberty is Thine.

Thy grace first made me feel my sin,
And taught me to believe,
Then, in believing, peace I found,
And now in Christ I live.

All that I am while here on earth,
All that I hope to be,
When Jesus comes and glory dawns,
I owe it, Lord, to Thee.

By Horatius Bonar 1808-1809

Chapter 15

Pillar 12

The Fifth Doctrine of Grace

"The Perseverance of the Saints"
(Or "The Perseverance of God with the Saints")

The logical conclusion of those who believe the Bible teaching that *"Salvation is of the LORD"* (Jonah 2:9) and absolutely no part of it is dependent upon any condition found in the elect sinner, but is wholly dependent upon the God who has willed to save those whom He gave to His dear Son - then it follows that salvation can never be lost. The saints of God will surely persevere unto the end because He has promised that no one and nothing in this universe or beyond it can take them away from Him. (John 10:28}

"My sheep hear My voice, and I know them, and they follow Me. And I give them eternal life, and they shall never perish; neither shall anyone snatch them out of My hand. My Father, who has given them to Me, is greater than all; and no one is able to snatch them out of My Father's hand."

John 10:27-29

Though we may temporarily fall into sin - we shall be granted the grace of repentance and shall persevere because He wills us to, and grants us the will to do so.

PERSEVERANCE DEPENDS ON GOD

Jude 24 *"Now unto Him Who is able to keep you from falling, and to present you faultless before the presence of His glory..."*

Jude 1 *"To those who are.... preserved in Christ Jesus and called.."*

Ezek.36:27 *"I WILL PUT my Spirit within you, and I WILL CAUSE you to walk in My statutes..."* See Ezek.11:19 Deut. 30:6

NOT DEPENDENT UPON THE ELECT

1 Pet.1:5 *"You (elect) are kept by the power of God."*

2 Tim 1:12 *"I know whom I have believed, and am persuaded that He is able to keep what I have committed unto Him until that Day."* (NKJV)

2 Tim 4:18 *"The Lord...will preserve me unto His heavenly kingdom."*

GOD WILLS THE SAINTS TO PERSEVERE UNTO THE END

Ps.37:28 *"For the LORD...does not forsake His saints, they are preserved forever."* (NKJV) I Thess.5:23,24 *"....be preserved blameless unto the coming of our Lord Jesus Christ. Faithful is He who calls you, who will also do it."*

Phil.1:6 *"Being confident of this very thing, that He who has begun a good work in you will perform it unto the day of Jesus Christ."*

THEREFORE SALVATION CANNOT BE LOST

John 6:37–39 *"All that the Father gives to Me will come to Me, and the one who comes to Me I will by no means cast out…This is the will of Him who sent Me, that of all He has given Me I should lose nothing, but should raise it up at the last day."* (NKJV)

John 6:39 *"This is the will of the Father Who sent me, that I shall lose none of all whom He has given me."*

John 10:27–29 As quoted above – No one can snatch us from the "double-grip" of the Father and the Son!

Read the second half of John Chapter 6. Also John 17:12, 18:9.

"Does God Wants To Save Everybody!" ??

One of the most popular misrepresentations of God in modern evangelism is that "God loves everyone equally, and wants to save everybody." This springs from a failure to understand the distinction between;

(a) The will of **Decree.** (God's sovereign efficacious* will - which nothing can resist)

(b) The will of **Demand.** (God's preceptive will - His precepts - commandments - which may be disobeyed) and

(c) The will of **Desire** (This refers to God's disposition). God's disposition is to love all men, but in His Holiness there are many that He also hates. A working knowledge of the Bible will reveal that there are many whom God, in His Holiness, justly and righteously hates. Indeed all unregenerate men are deserving of His hatred and wrath - for all have sinned.

The Lord tests the righteous,
But the wicked and the one who loves violence His soul hates.
Upon the wicked He will rain coals;
Fire and brimstone and a burning wind
Shall be the portion of their cup.
For the Lord is righteous,
He loves righteousness;
His countenance beholds the upright.
Psalm 11:5-7

"It is written: Jacob have I loved, but Esau have I hated." Rom.9:13

Ask yourself such questions as "Who is it that will never perish, in John 3:16 ?

Ans. "Whoever believes.

Q. Who are these believers?

Ans. Elect believers.

If God decreed that none should perish, then none would perish! - all would come to repentance.

2 Peter 3:9 and other texts like it, must refer to God's loving disposition, not to what He has purposed from before the foundation of the world - He purposed to set his particular love on **some** undeserving sinners from among mankind, and provide for their salvation by His **decree** before the world was created.

Assurance of Salvation

This final Doctrine of Grace – the "P" of TULIP, is important for us in relation to the **assurance** we should have regarding our salvation by grace alone, through faith alone, in the 'finished work' of Christ alone.

The phrase, "Once saved, always saved" is frequently quoted by evangelical Christians. It tells a truth. But only for those who are **truly** saved by grace . (Going forward at the invitation of a preacher and saying a prayer – however sincerely – will not save you. Indeed it may give you a false assurance of salvation.)

Those who have been drawn to Christ and have put their trust in His substitutionary[7] death and resurrection, **may know for sure** that they will persevere unto the end. Because God will persevere in completing their salvation.

"...being confident of this very thing, that He who has begun a good work in you will complete it until the day of Jesus Christ;" Philippians 1:6

Every believer can and should have assurance of salvation.

"My sheep hear My voice, and I know them, and they follow Me. And I give them eternal life, and they shall never perish;,"

John 10:27

---

[7] Substitutionary – that is, as a substitute. To be able to say that Christ died in **my** place and paid the penalty for **my** sin. When He died, I died. When He rose again, I rose again in Him.

Hymn

'Blessed assurance, Jesus is mine;
Oh, what a foretaste of glory divine!
Heir of salvation, purchase of God,
Born of His Spirit, washed in His blood.

This is my story, this is my song,
Praising my Saviour all the day long.
This is my story, this is my song,
Praising my Saviour all the day long.

Perfect submission, perfect delight,
Visions of rapture now burst on my sight;
Angels descending, bring from above
Echoes of mercy, whispers of love.

This is my story…..

Perfect submission, all is at rest,
I in my Saviour am happy and blest;
Watching and waiting, looking above,
Filled with His goodness, lost in His love.

This is my story…..

By Frances Jane van Alstyne commonly known as Fanny Crosby 1829-1915

Fanny Crosby was an American Rescue Mission worker who wrote more than 8,000 Hymns with more than 100million copies printed, despite being blind from shortly after birth. Another great hymn she wrote was "To God be the glory".

Chapter 16

Conclusion

WHY THE MESSAGE OF THIS BOOK IS SO IMPORTANT

We believe that this message is important for the salvation of souls in an age when many are being led to think that they are Christians when in fact they are deceived or mistaken. The result is that the whole church is weakened and the Gospel is brought into disrepute.

For example, the "invitation" method used in much modern (so-called) evangelism is based on an 'Arminian' view of the Gospel. In that view, Salvation ultimately depends on what YOU as an unregenerate sinner must do. The teaching is that YOU must believe in order to be "born again". However, through the preaching of the true **Gospel of Grace**, men and women are first "born again" - and then as a **result** of their new birth they will respond with true repentance and faith in the Lord Jesus Christ. The difference is crucial! The first depends on man's supposed 'free will' the second wholly upon the grace of God and man has nothing in which to boast!

....*"He chose us in Him before the foundation of the world, that we should be holy and without blame before Him in love, having predestined us to adoption as sons by Jesus Christ to Himself, according to the good pleasure of His will, to the praise of the glory of His grace, by which he has made us accepted in the beloved."* Ephesians 1:4–6

"For by grace you have been saved through faith, and that not of yourselves; it is the gift of God, not of works, lest anyone should boast." Ephesians 2:8.9

All Twelve Pillars - The Sovereignty of God, the Gospel of Grace, the Five 'Solas' and the Five Doctrines of Grace may not be understood by all true believers. They may have lacked teachers. Or, they may have been taught wrongly. But Jesus promised that the Holy Spirit would lead us into all truth. So if these 12 Pillars are indeed what the Bible teaches (and I and many others are fully convinced that they are), then all who are born-again of the Spirit of God will, when learning the truths they express, embrace them. Then as true disciples they will share them as integral with the one true gospel of the gracious salvation they have in Christ Jesus.

In the Introduction in Chapter 1, we asked the following:

A Key Question

If you were to die tonight and found yourself before God – and God asked you **"Why should I let you into my heaven?"** How would you answer?

You might want to give a very different answer now that you have read this book than you might have given before you read it.

No way are you going to try to justify your right to enter heaven as a result of your good works. Or that you have "done your best". Or that you have been religious – going to church, saying prayers, receiving sacraments, having been baptised etc.. Or even that you responded to a "gospel invitation" and "gave your heart to Jesus" at some point in your life!

This is how Jesus concludes His "Sermon on the Mount" as recorded in Matthew's Gospel:

"Not everyone who says to Me, 'Lord, Lord,' shall enter the kingdom of heaven, but he who does the will of My Father in

heaven. Many will say to Me in that day, 'Lord, Lord, have we not prophesied in Your name, cast out demons in Your name, and done many wonders in Your name?' And then I will declare to them, 'I never knew you; depart from Me, you who practice lawlessness!'

"Therefore whoever hears these sayings of Mine, and does them, I will liken him to a wise man who built his house on the rock: and the rain descended, the floods came, and the winds blew and beat on that house; and it did not fall, for it was founded on the rock.

"But everyone who hears these sayings of Mine, and does not do them, will be like a foolish man who built his house on the sand: and the rain descended, the floods came, and the winds blew and beat on that house; and it fell. And great was its fall."
Matthew 7:21-27

We trust that you would now Answer that **Key Question** and answer it clearly:

"Because, Father, You are a holy and just God. You gave Your Son to die on the cross in my place. I am trusting that He paid for all my sins. . His shed blood is now my only plea.

You look on me now as your son / daughter, washed in His blood and clothed in His righteousness. Thank You for the free gift of salvation to sinners like me.

Hymn – Amazing Grace

Amazing grace! How sweet the sound
that saved a wretch like me!
I once was lost, but now am found,
was blind, but now I see.

'Twas grace first taught my heart to fear
and grace my fears relieved;
how precious did that grace appear
the hour I first believed!

My rebel soul, that once withstood
the Saviour's kindest call,
rejoices now, by grace subdued,
to serve him with its all.

Through many dangers, toils and snares
I have already come;
God's grace has brought me safe thus far,
and grace will lead me home.

The Lord has promised good to me,
his word my hope secures;
he will my shield and portion be
as long as life endures.

Yes, when this heart and flesh shall fail
and mortal life shall cease,
I shall possess within the veil
a life of joy and peace.

What thanks I owe you, and what love-
a boundless, endless store-
shall echo through the realms above
when time shall be no more.

The earth shall soon dissolve like snow,
the sun forbear to shine;
but God, who called me here below,
will be forever mine.

When we've been there ten thousand years
bright shining as the sun,
we've no less days to sing God's praise
than when we first begun.

Amen

Original Hymn by John Newton (1725–1807) Former Slave Trader Converted to Preacher of the Gospel of Grace. Some verses added later. This is reputed to be the most famous Christian Hymn of all time.

Appendix A

A General Statement of Faith

We believe the Bible to be the inspired, the only infallible, authoritative Word of God.

We believe that there is one God, eternally existent in three persons: Father, Son, and the Holy Spirit.

We believe in the deity of our Lord Jesus Christ, in His virgin birth, in His sinless life, in His miracles, in His vicarious sufferings and atoning death through His shed blood, in His bodily resurrection, in His ascension to the right hand of the Father, and in His personal future return in power and glory.

We believe that for the salvation of lost and sinful man, regeneration (new birth) by the Holy Spirit is absolutely essential.

We believe in the present ministry of the Holy Spirit by whose indwelling the Christian is enabled to live a godly life.

We believe in the resurrection of both the saved and the lost; they that are saved unto the resurrection of life and they that are lost unto the resurrection of damnation.

We believe in the spiritual unity of all 'born-again' believers in our Lord Jesus Christ.

The Lord Jesus Christ, immediately before He returned to heaven, commanded His disciples to proclaim the Gospel throughout the world and to disciple people from every nation; baptising them and teaching them everything Jesus had taught them. (Matthew 28:18-20)

The fulfilment of that 'Great Commission' requires the involvement and commitment of **every** believer. This is the primary mission of the church.

Appendix B

Some Definitions:

Atonement - to make amends for - from 'at-one-ment' - to make reconciliation, to make one.

Substitutionary – as a substitute Christ suffered and died in the place of elect sinners. – as their substitute, paying the penalty for their sins.

Attributes - characteristics, qualities. Nature

Baptism - This word in almost all English Bibles has been copied from the Greek word used in New Testament – 'baptiso'. In other words, it was transliterated rather then translated. The simplest translation is: ' immersion '. Depending on the context, it means immersed in water, or in the Spirit, or in the body of Christ.

Efficacious - effective in its working

Infallibility - not able to fail or be wrong

Omnipotent – Having all power, Almighty

Omniscient - Knowing absolutely everything, past present and future.

Predestination - to destine beforehand, making the end certain. from the beginning

Redemption To redeem, in Bible times often referred to paying a price to set a slave free. Jesus came to redeem elect sinners – pay the price of their sins and set them free from the power and effect of sin.

Sacraments - from the Latin, to make something holy. It refers to how (it is supposed) in Baptism and the Lord's Supper, the outward signs (automatically) convey inward grace. – water, bread, wine, being blessed, (they suppose) become means of grace – ways in which grace is administered or conveyed. Protestants kept these two, the Church of Rome maintained a further five sacraments including marriage, ordination and confession of sins to a priest.

Synergism Two forces operating or working together .(Heresy - means false doctrine) Salvation is not a joint effort. It is 'monergistic' – a single force working alone.

Monergism A single working force or energy.

Justification – to justify is to make just. We are accounted righteous – therefore just, acquitted of lawless acts in the sight of God. We are justified by faith alone. This is justification. This was the doctrine rediscovered which sparked the Reformation in the 15th and 16th Century.

Appendix C

The Sovereignty Of God

A Collection of Scriptures on this topic

These Bible quotations are mostly from the King James (Authorised) Version:

(Genesis 18:14) "Is any thing too hard for the LORD? At the time appointed I will return unto thee, according to the time of life, and Sarah shall have a son."

(Exodus 33:18-19) "And he said, I beseech thee, show me thy glory. {19} And he said, I will make all my goodness pass before thee, and I will proclaim the name of the LORD before thee; and will be gracious to whom I will be gracious, and will show mercy on whom I will show mercy."

(Job 42:1-2) Then Job answered the LORD, and said, "I know that thou canst do every thing, and that no thought can be withheld from thee."

(Psalms 115:3) "But our God *is* in the heavens: he has done whatsoever he has pleased."

(Psalms 135:6) "Whatsoever the LORD pleased, *that* did he in heaven, and in earth, in the seas, and all deep places."

(Isaiah 14:24) "The LORD of hosts hath sworn, saying, Surely as I have thought, so shall it come to pass; and as I have purposed, *so* shall it stand:"

(Isaiah 14:27) "For the LORD of hosts has purposed, and who shall disannul *it?* And his hand *is* stretched out, and who shall turn it back?"

(Isaiah 40:12-25) "Who has measured the waters in the hollow of his hand, and meted out heaven with the span, and comprehended the dust of the earth in a measure, and weighed the mountains in scales, and the hills in a balance? {13} Who has directed the Spirit of the LORD, or *being* his counsellor has taught him? {14} With whom took he counsel, and *who* instructed him, and taught him in the path of judgment, and taught him knowledge, and showed to him the way of understanding? *{15}* Behold, the nations *are* as a drop in a bucket, and are counted as the small dust of the balance: behold, he takes up the isles as a very little thing. *{16}* And Lebanon *is* not sufficient to burn, nor the beasts thereof sufficient for a burnt offering. *{17}* All nations before him *are* as nothing; and they are counted to him less than nothing, and vanity. *{18}* To whom then will ye liken God? Or what likeness will ye compare unto him? *{19}* The workman melts a graven image, and the goldsmith spreads it over with gold, and casts silver chains. *{20}* He that *is* so impoverished that he hath no oblation chooses a tree *that* will not rot; he seeks unto him a cunning workman to prepare a graven image, *that* shall not be moved. *{21}* Have ye not known? Have ye not heard? Hath it not been told you from the beginning? Have ye not understood from the foundations of the earth? *{22}* *It is* he that sits upon the circle of the earth, and the inhabitants thereof *are* as grasshoppers; that stretches out the heavens as a curtain, and spreads them out as a tent to dwell in: *{23}* That brings the princes to nothing; he makes the judges of the earth as vanity. *{24}* Yea, they shall not be planted; yea, they shall not be sown: yea, their stock shall not take root in the earth: and he shall also blow upon them, and they shall wither, and the whirlwind shall take them away as stubble. *{25}* To whom then will ye liken me, or shall I be equal? Says the Holy One."

(Isaiah 46:9-11) "Remember the former things of old: for I *am* God, and *there is* none else; *I am* God, and *there is* none like me, *{10}* Declaring the end from the beginning, and from ancient times *the things* that are not *yet* done, saying, My counsel shall stand, and I will do all my pleasure: *{11}* Calling a ravenous bird from the east, the man that executes my counsel from a far country: yea, I have spoken *it,* I will also bring it to pass; I have purposed *it,* I will also do it."

(Isaiah 55:11) "So shall my word be that goes forth out of my mouth: it shall not return unto me void, but it shall accomplish that which I please, and it shall prosper *in the thing* whereto I sent it."

(Jeremiah 32:17) "Ah Lord GOD! Behold, thou hast made the heaven and the earth by thy great power and stretched out arm, *and* there is nothing too hard for thee:"

(Lamentations 3:37) "Who *is* he *that* says, and it comes to pass, *when* the Lord commands *it* not?"

(Daniel 4:34-37) "And at the end of the days I Nebuchadnezzar lifted up mine eyes unto heaven, and mine understanding returned unto me, and I blessed the most High, and I praised and honoured him that lives for ever, whose dominion *is* an everlasting dominion, and his kingdom *is* from generation to generation: *{35}* And all the inhabitants of the earth *are* reputed as nothing: and he doeth according to his will in the army of heaven, and *among* the inhabitants of the earth: and none can stay his hand, or say unto him, What doest thou? *{36}* At the same time my reason returned unto me; and for the glory of my kingdom, mine honour and brightness returned unto me; and my counsellors and my lords sought unto me; and I was established in my kingdom, and excellent majesty was added unto me. *{37}* Now I Nebuchadnezzar praise and extol and honour the King of heaven, all whose works *are* truth, and his ways judgment: and those that walk in pride he is able to abase."

(Matthew 11:20-27) "Then began he to upbraid the cities wherein most of his mighty works were done, because they repented not: *{21}* Woe unto thee, Chorazin! woe unto thee, Bethsaida! for if the mighty works, which were done in you, had been done in Tyre and Sidon, they would have repented long ago in sackcloth and ashes. *{22}* But I say unto you, It shall be more tolerable for Tyre and Sidon at the day of judgment, than for you. *{23}* And thou, Capernaum, which art exalted unto heaven, shalt be brought down to hell: for if the mighty works, which have been done in thee, had been done in Sodom, it would have remained until this day. *{24}* But I say unto you, That it shall be more tolerable for the land of Sodom in the day of judgment, than for thee. {25} At that time Jesus answered and said, I thank thee, O Father, Lord of heaven and earth, because thou hast hid these things from the wise and prudent, and hast revealed them unto babes. {26} Even so, Father: for so it seemed good in thy sight. {27} All things are delivered unto me of my Father: and no man knows the Son, but the Father; neither knows any man the Father, save the Son, and *he* to whomsoever the Son will reveal *him.*"

(Matthew 28:18) "And Jesus came and spoke to them, saying, All power is given unto me in heaven and in earth."

(Romans 9:20-24) "Nay but, O man, who art thou that repliest against God? Shall the thing formed say to him that formed *it,* Why hast thou made me thus? {21} Hath not the potter power over the clay, of the same lump to make one vessel unto honour, and another unto dishonour? {22} *What* if God, willing to show *his* wrath, and to make his power known, endured with much longsuffering the vessels of wrath fitted to destruction: {23} And that he might make known the riches of his glory on the vessels of mercy, which he had afore prepared unto glory, {24} Even us, whom he hath called, not of the Jews only, but also of the Gentiles?"

(Ephesians 1:11) "In whom also we have obtained an inheritance, being predestined according to the purpose of him who works all things after the counsel of his own will:"

(Ephesians 1:22) "And hath put all *things* under his feet, and gave him *to be* the head over all *things* to the church,"

There are many other passages of Scripture that could be included that refer to God's sovereignty, but the above quotations should prove more than sufficient.

This doctrine is where we started and it is where we finish. He is the Alpha and Omega, the beginning and the end. **To Him be all the glory!**

The Author

Fred Serjeant has been married to Mary for 60 years and they have three sons, six grandchildren and have one great grandson. Fred has been in pastoral and evangelistic ministry for 65 years, He is the author of three other books published through Amazon:

"Understanding the New Covenant" A Simple Introduction to New Covenant Theology

"Make Disciples!". Making Disciples who make Disciples – A Discipleship Manaual.

"12 Steps Out – A manual for Freedom from Addiction"
All available in Paperback and Kindle versions at amazon.co.uk or amazon.com

----

Note from the Author:
I trust that this book will be helpful especially in discipling new believers. In the book mentioned above – Make Disciple! I

endeavour to point out that effective evangelism is through disciples making disciples who make further disciples.

If this book is a help in doing that, then please pass copies on to others who might do the same!

If you have any questions about the teaching in this book which you would like to ask me (the author), please go to my website at: www.simplechurch.org.uk
 Facebook: Frederick Serjeant Twitter: @FredSerjeant
or email me at f.serjeant@gmail.com

(D.V. Provided I am still in this world!)

Made in the USA
Columbia, SC
30 August 2022

66318367R00078